CLANG!

by MARK WEAKLAND
illustrated by LOIC BILLIAU

WILE E. COYOTE
EXPERIMENTS WITH
MAGNETISM

CAPSTONE PRESS
a capstone imprint

Published in 2017 by Capstone Press
A Capstone Imprint
1710 Roe Crest Drive
North Mankato, Minnesota 56003
www.mycapstone.com

Library of Congress Cataloging-in-Publication Data
Names: Weakland, Mark, author. | Billiau, Loic, illustrator.
Title: Clang! : Wile E. Coyote experiments with magnetism / by Mark Weakland;
illustrated by Loic Billiau.
Description: North Mankato, Minnesota : Capstone Press, 2017. | Series:
Warner Brothers. Wile E. Coyote, physical science genius | Audience: Ages 8–12. | Audience: Grades
4 to 6. | Includes bibliographical references and index.
Identifiers: LCCN 2016045597| ISBN 9781515737315 (library binding) | ISBN 9781515737353 (pbk.) |
ISBN 9781515737476 (ebook pdf)
Subjects: LCSH: Magnetism—Experiments—Juvenile literature. | Science—Experiments—Juvenile
literature. | Wile E. Coyote (Fictitious character)—Juvenile literature.
Classification: LCC QC753.7 .W387 2017 | DDC 538.078—dc23
LC record available at https://lccn.loc.gov/2016045597

Editorial Credits
Michelle Hasselius, editor; Ashlee Suker, designer; Steve Walker, production specialist

Capstone Press thanks Paul Ohmann, PhD, Associate Professor of Physics at the
University of St. Thomas for his help creating this book.

Printed and bound in the USA.
010057S17CG

TABLE OF CONTENTS

Magnets Attract!

Poor Wile E. Coyote. He tries so hard to attract success, but all he gets is trouble. Maybe Wile E. should study the science of magnets. If he understood what they are and how they work, catching Road Runner might not be so painful.

Coyote
(Hungrius carnivorii)

Road Runner
(Speedius birdius)

A magnet is any object that produces an invisible **magnetic field**. Some magnets are shaped like bars. Some are shaped like horseshoes. Some magnets are small and some are large. A magnet's magnetic field **attracts** certain substances. But a feather is not one of them. No matter the size or shape, a magnet will never attract a bird. But a steel sign? Yes!

CLANG!

magnetic field—a region of space near a magnet or electric current in which a magnetic force can act on an object

attract—to pull something toward something else

CHAPTER 1

FIELD DAY

Lodestones

Most magnets are manufactured, but a few occur in nature. These natural magnets are called lodestones. Lodestones can be found in rocks lying on the ground. Wile E. is learning about them the hard way.

Magnets are made of metal. Most are made of iron. Heavy and gray, iron is the most commonly found metal on Earth. Iron is found in many places, including rocks.

Scientists think lightning could create lodestones. A bolt of lighting produces a strong electric current. The current creates a powerful magnetic field. If a rock is struck by lightning, it comes in contact with the magnetic field. The iron in the rock would be permanently magnetized. This would create a natural magnet.

Lodestones can be hard to find. But Wile E. has found one. What a lucky coyote!

Magnets and Iron

Magnetic force attracts all kinds of objects. Wile E. learned this when his magnet pulled that road sign out of the ground. The sign was made of steel, which is a blend of iron and other metals.

IRON BBs
ACME

BIRD SEED +
IRON BBs

BIRD SEED
ACME

Magnets don't attract everything. They won't attract wooden pencils, plastic toys, gold bracelets, or silver chains. But they will attract objects made with iron. Metal desks, refrigerator doors, nails, paper clips, and steel BBs all contain iron. Too bad those BBs aren't inside Road Runner!

Magnetic Fields

A magnet's power comes from its invisible magnetic field. The field produces the force that pushes and pulls on objects. But if the field is invisible, how can Wile E. be sure it is there?

ACME
IRON FILINGS

ACME
BIG BAR MAGNET

BIG BAR MAGNET

GIANT SKILLET   FIRE PIT

To see the magnetic field around his magnet, Wile E. scatters small pieces of iron. These tiny iron flakes are called iron filings. The filings line up in the direction of the magnetic field. Filings make it possible to see how the invisible field surrounds the magnet.

There is a lot of force coming from this magnet. Wile E. thinks it's strong enough to pull his iron skillet into the fire. Let's find out if he's right.

ACME
IRON FILINGS

N S

BIG BAR
MAGNET

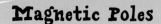 # OPPOSITES ATTRACT

Magnetic Poles

Magnets have **polarity**. Polarity means there are two things opposing each other. A magnet's power is strongest at its two ends. This is easy to see in a bar magnet, which is a straight piece of magnetized iron.

The two ends of a bar magnet are called **poles**. They are typically named the north pole and the south pole.

Wile E. plans to use his magnet to pull Road Runner. Will his plan work?

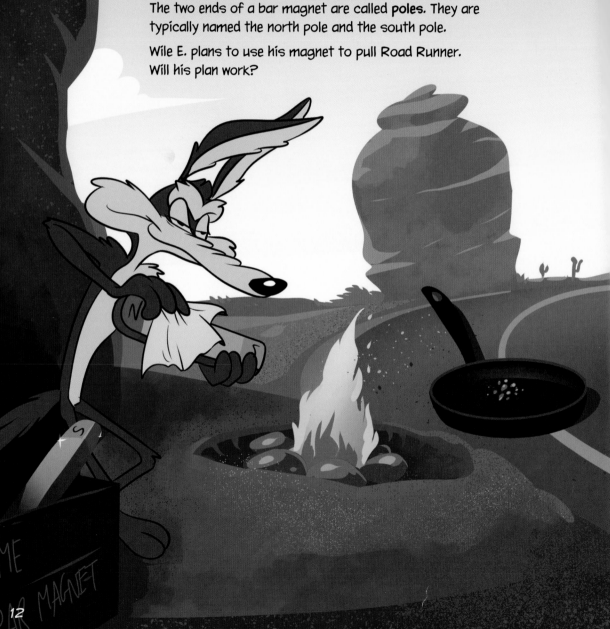

Earth is like a giant magnet. It has a solid iron core in the center that is surrounded by hot liquid rock, which also contains iron. As the iron in the liquid rock moves around the iron core, a magnetic field is created. Like all magnets, Earth has a north and south pole. Earth's magnetic north pole points toward the south. The magnetic south pole points toward the north.

polarity—having two oppositely charged poles; one end of a magnet is called the north pole and the other end is called the south pole

pole—either of the two regions or parts of a magnet that exhibits magnetic polarity

Poles Attract and Repel

Magnets can attract or repel. Opposite poles of a magnet attract. A north pole attracts a south pole. Poor Wile E. is experiencing that right now!

repel—to exert a force on an object so that the object is pushed away

Matching poles repel each other. A south pole repels another south pole. In fact, it's almost impossible to make them touch! It looks like Wile E.'s life would be easier with magnets that repel instead of attract.

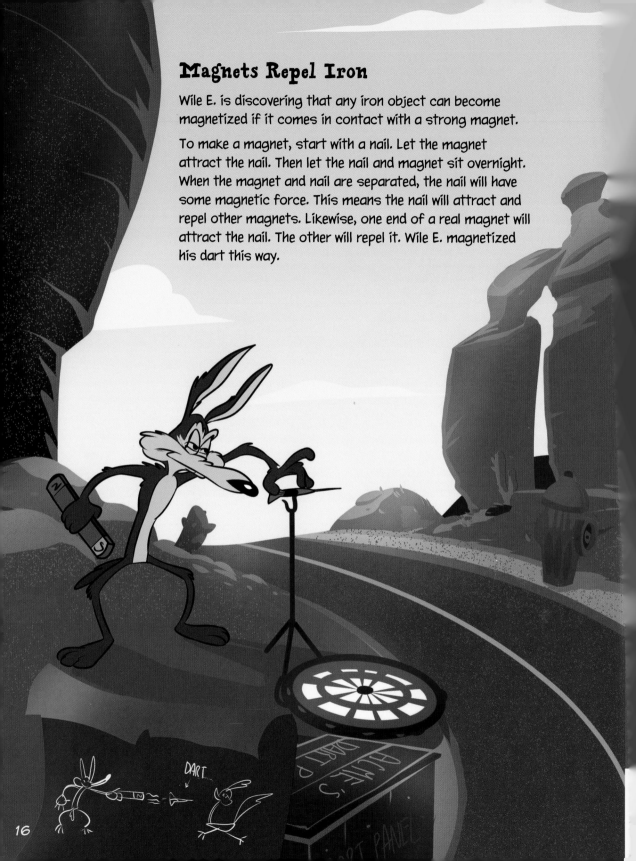

Magnets Repel Iron

Wile E. is discovering that any iron object can become magnetized if it comes in contact with a strong magnet.

To make a magnet, start with a nail. Let the magnet attract the nail. Then let the nail and magnet sit overnight. When the magnet and nail are separated, the nail will have some magnetic force. This means the nail will attract and repel other magnets. Likewise, one end of a real magnet will attract the nail. The other will repel it. Wile E. magnetized his dart this way.

Wile E.'s plan might have worked if the Road Runner hadn't ducked. But he did. Plus, Wile E. forgot about the iron fire hydrant. Now his plan for capturing Road Runner is all washed up!

CHAPTER 3

AN ELECTRIFYING EXPERIENCE

Electricity and Magnetism

With his glasses and big book, Wile E. looks pretty smart right now. He is reading all about electricity and magnetism. Wile E. is learning that they are a lot alike. Check out his chart that compares the two.

Electricity	Magnetism
positive and negative charges	north and south poles
opposite charges attract	opposite poles attract
matching charges repel	matching poles repel
fields form around the charges	fields form around the poles
electric field comes from charges	magnetic field comes from moving charges

Because electricity and magnetism are related, Wile E. can make a special magnet. It's called an **electromagnet**. For a genius like Wile E., making one is easy. All he needs is wire, electricity, and a quiet place to work.

electromagnet—a device consisting of an iron or steel core that is magnetized by an electric current in a coil that surrounds it

Creating a Magnetic Field

He's done it! Wile E. has made an electromagnet. Next step? Capture Road Runner!

Like electric fields, magnetic fields are created with **charges**. But magnetic fields come from moving charges called an electric **current**. In a permanent magnet, a magnetic field is created from the movement of **electrons** inside the magnet. But in an electromagnet, the field comes from charges flowing along a wire.

To build an electromagnet, Wile E. wraps a long wire around a nail. Then he attaches an energy source—a battery. When he throws the switch, energy flows through the wire. The current creates a magnetic field.

With his switch, Wile E. can turn his magnet on and off. What magnet tricks will he perform next?

charge—the amount of electricity moving through something

current—the flow of electric charges

electron—one of the tiny particles that make up all things

Electromagnets

Wile E.'s magnet gun is made from wire wrapped around an iron bar. When a current flows through the wire, a magnetic field forms around the wire. This magnetizes the iron bar. Now it acts like a magnet. The strength of the magnetic field depends on the number of coils in the wire.

To build a strong magnet, Wile E. wraps the wire around and around the bar. Now he hopes to pull anything metal to him, even a heavy steel cage.

Wait a minute ... nothing is happening. It looks like Wile E.'s magnet gun isn't strong enough. To fix the problem, he could add more wire. He could add more electricity. Or he could do both. More wire and more electricity will certainly make Wile E.'s magnet more powerful.

More Electromagnets

Wile E.'s small magnet gun wasn't strong enough to attract the cage. But his new, giant magnet gun should do the trick.

More powerful electromagnets can be made by wrapping lots of wire. But more than wire is needed. To make a magnet as powerful as possible, an electric current is needed. Lots of it. When more electric current flows, a stronger magnetic field is created.

Powerful electromagnets attract all kinds of iron objects. In a scrapyard, an electromagnet can lift more than 2,000 pounds (907 kilograms) of scrap metal at a time.

Wile E.'s magnet is working well—too well. Poor Wile E.! He fails even when he succeeds.

Magnets in Motors

It's up, up, and away. To capture Road Runner, Wile E. is test-driving his new electric motor flying machine.

Electric motors are everywhere. They spin ceiling fans, power toy trains, and turn the beaters on electric mixers. Inside each motor is a set of magnets. Each magnet generates a magnetic field. The two fields attract and repel one another in a constant cycle. This cycle can be turned into motion. Here's how:

Wile E. wraps a **rotor** in wire. A current flows through the wire, creating a magnetic field. A magnet is on both sides of the rotor. Each magnet's poles alternately attract and repel each other. This makes the rotor spin on its axle.

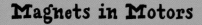

N S

TO BATTERY

BRUSHES

AXLE

ARMATURE

FIELD   MAGNET!

rotor—a rotating part of a machine

A motor's spinning axle does a lot of work. Attach beaters to it, and the motor will mix brownie batter. Put helicopter rotors on it, and the motor will lift a coyote into the air. But Wile E. has forgotten one important thing—electric motors only run when there is electricity!

Magnets Matter

Wile E.'s magnetic plans never worked. Road Runner is still on the loose, racing up and down the roads. And Wile E. is still chasing Road Runner with his knife and fork.

Even though his plans failed, Wile E. learned a lot about magnets. Now he knows they attract and repel objects made of iron. He knows that all magnets have a magnetic field and two poles, one north and one south. And Wile E. understands that magnetism is related to electricity. Because the two are related, wire and electricity can be used to make an electromagnet.

Maybe Road Runner is like a magnet. Why else would Wile E. Coyote be so attracted to him?

GLOSSARY

attract (uh-TRAKT)—to pull something toward something else

charge (CHARJ)—the amount of electricity moving through something

current (KUHR-uhnt)—the flow of electric charges

electromagnet (i-lek-troh-MAG-nuht)—a device consisting of an iron or steel core that is magnetized by electric current in a coil that surrounds it

electron (i-LEK-tron)—one of the tiny particles that make up all things

magnetic field (mag-NET-ik FEELD)—a region of space near a magnet or electric current in which a magnetic force can act on another substance

polarity (poh-LAYR-uh-dee)—having two oppositely charged poles

pole (POHL)—either of the two regions or parts of a magnet that exhibits magnetic polarity

repel (ri-PEL)—to exert a force on an object so that the object is pushed away

rotor (ROH-tur)—a rotating part of a machine

READ MORE

Kessler, Colleen. *A Project Guide to Electricity and Magnetism.* Physical Science Projects for Kids. Hockessin, Del.: Mitchell Lane, 2012.

Swanson, Jennifer. *The Attractive Truth About Magnetism.* LOL Physical Science. North Mankato, Minn.: Capstone Press, 2013.

Troupe, Thomas Kingsley. *Magnet Power!: Science Adventures with MAG-3000 the Origami Robot.* Origami Science Adventures. North Mankato, Minn.: Picture Window Books, 2013.

INTERNET SITES

FactHound offers a safe, fun way to find Internet sites related to this book. All of the sites on FactHound have been researched by our staff.

Here's all you do:

Visit *www.facthound.com*

Type in this code: 9781515737315

Check out projects, games and lots more at
www.capstonekids.com

INDEX

OTHER BOOKS IN THIS SERIES